**Printed and published in Great Britain by D.C. THOMSON & Co., Ltd.,
185 Fleet Street, London. © D.C. THOMSON & Co., Ltd., 1997.**
(Certain stories do not appear exactly as originally published.)
ISBN 0-85116-636-9

THE COMICS at CHRISTMAS

The Beano has occasionally given its readers their very own Christmas cards, printed in an issue leading up to Christmas. These are four examples from the 1960s, to prepare you readers for the sackfuls of laughter in this first, pre-Christmas, section.

Minnie the Minx

Back in 1960, Minnie the Minx couldn't wait to open her presents, but left herself open to a few problems!

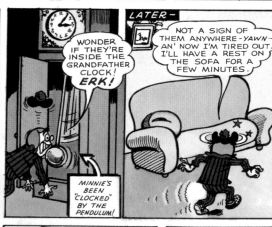

BRASSNECK

IT was Christmas Eve and Chuckler Charley Brand wondered why his amazing metal pal was so quiet. He went off to see—and found Brassneck book-worming through a book.

COME ON, BRASSNECK! LET'S HAVE A SNOWBALL FIGHT!

A CHRISTMAS CAROL

The pals were having great fun when suddenly a snow-ball hit a doorbell.

TAKE THAT!

MISSED!

EBENEZER SCROUNGER SOLICITOR

RING

Old Ebenezer Scrounger came to the door—and promptly got the next snowball on the beak.

WHO RANG MY BELL?

WOW!

WHIZZ!

OOF!

HA-HA! HO-HO!

I'LL GET YOU SCOUNDRELS FOR THAT! I'VE MEMORISED YOUR FACES!

Inside the office, Ebenezer's clerk, Rab Scratchit, roared with laughter.

Ebenezer was furious and he punished Rab for his mirth.

AND AS FOR YOU, RAB SCRATCHIT! YOU'LL GET NO CHRISTMAS HOLIDAY TOMORROW FOR LAUGHING AT ME!

Y-Y-YES, SIR!

Meanwhile, Charley and Brassneck had come upon a little cripple lad being snowballed by a bullying gang.

HELP!

HAW-HAW!

HEY! YOU BULLIES! LEAVE THAT LITTLE LAD ALONE!

Brassneck hoisted up the huge ball of snow he had been rolling—

—And hurled it at the bullies.

WHOOPEE! BULL'S-EYE, BRASSNECK!

OOF!

EEK!

ARGH!

Charley and Brassneck made friends with the cripple boy, whose name was Tiny Jim.

I'M GOING TO MEET MY DAD AT THE OFFICE!

COME ON. WE'LL MAKE SURE YOU GET THERE SAFELY!

With Tiny Jim hanging on to Brassneck's shoulders, the metal lad went sliding down the hill.

OH, BOY! THIS IS SMASHING!

WE KNOW ALL THE SHORT CUTS!

It turned out that Tiny Jim's father was Rab Scratchit.

HELLO, FATHER.

HELLO, TINY JIM!

REMEMBER, SCRATCHIT! DON'T BE LATE TOMORROW!

Mr Scratchit told Tiny Jim the bad news.

I'VE BAD NEWS FOR YOU, SON! I'M NOT GETTING A HOLIDAY TOMORROW.

THAT NIGHT

Charley planned to have revenge on old Scrounger for his meanness.

HOLD STILL WHILE I PAINT YOUR FACE WITH LUMINOUS PAINT, BRASSNECK!

LUMINOUS PAINT

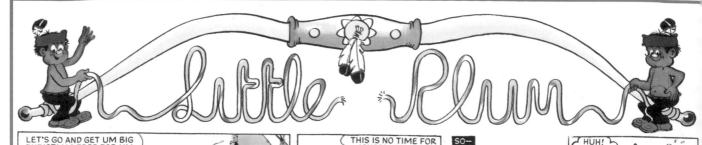

the DODGER

...e Beano's Roger the Dodger is more likely to pull a fast one than
...ll a cracker at Christmas! Here's an elemen'tree' dodge
... prove it!

HEE! THIS IS MORE IN LINE. NOW I CAN HAVE A LITTLE SNOOZE ON THE WAY HOME!

BUT TWO MILES FURTHER ON—

Z-Z-Z-Z-Z!

OHO! A STOWAWAY!

JUST AS I EXPECTED! THE DODGER HIMSELF! GET OFF AND WALK!

NO TREE FELLING

HOI!

...D, AT THE POLICE STATION—

...AT WAS THE BOY'S TREE YOU ...FTED! TAKE IT BACK AT ...NCE AND APOLOGISE!

YES, SIR!

15 MINUTES LATER—

H'M!

I-I'M S-SORRY, SIR—HONEST! IT WAS ALL A MISTAKE—GULP!

WHAT A DODGE, EH? THAT POOR OLD COP HAD TO CARRY MY TREE HOME FOR ME.

A FINE TIME TO WRENCH YOUR LEG AND SPRAIN YOUR ARM!

DODGE!

NOW YOU WON'T BE ABLE TO JOIN IN THE FUN AND GAMES AT YOUR CHRISTMAS EVE PARTY TONIGHT.

NO, DAD!

—WHICH IS JUST WHAT ROGER WANTED!

PLAYING ENERGETIC GAMES AND PULLING TOUGH CRACKERS IS TOO MUCH LIKE HARD WORK! THIS IS MORE IN MY LINE!

PUFF!

GASP!

CHOCS

OUR HA-HA-HAPPY XMAS NUMBER

THE BEANO

EVERY THURSDAY

No. 649. DEC. 25th, 1954.

2ᴰ

DANNY LONGLEGS

IT was Christmas Eve, and the snow fell thick and fast, the way it always did in these good old days. Danny Long was chilly, but still cheery, for this strange crowd of Easterners who held him prisoner felt the cold worse than he did. The weather got all of them down — all but one. That one was their leader, His Most Elevated Highness Prince Ali Khan, who stayed up high on his throne because of his royal rule that his head must be higher than anyone else's.

2 — Longlegs was being taken by the Easterners to join the Giant Bodyguard of the Great Khan. Already he was far from Sleepy Valley but he still had high hopes of getting free. His hopes had to be high, for he was over ten feet tall! Anyway, Danny's plan was to make himself such a nuisance that the Prince would be glad to get rid of him. A chance came to Danny at night. The Easterners were almost frozen stiff, so Longlegs made a fire of Prince Ali's huge royal bed!

3 — Prince's men were glad of the heat — but Prince Ali wasn't so glad when he found out what was burning. He raved and raged, and then since there was nowhere for him to sleep he gave orders to march on. That was how it came about that they reached a huge turreted castle where the Prince commanded that food and shelter should be sought. There was no-one around so Danny led the way inside.

4 — A strange scene met their gaze in the big hall of the castle. There wasn't a single article of furniture on the stone-flagged floor. Tables and chairs were slung up by ropes near the ceiling. Other ropes with metal rings on them hung right along the hall. As Danny looked around, an armoured knight came lumbering towards him — walking on stilts! "Welcome to Rathole Towers!" he boomed out through his helmet.

5 — The knight, Sir Toby Belch, quickly explained the queer state of affairs in his castle. "The place is overrun with rats," he said. "Hundreds of rats, so big and fat that they've killed off all the cats. I have to sleep in armour to avoid being eaten myself! Just watch what happens when my servants bring in some food." Sir Toby called his men, and the Prince was entertained to the queerest feast he had ever eaten.

6 — The servants either walked on stilts or climbed ropes as they spread the mid-air table. Sir Toby and Prince Ali sat on the hanging chairs. But the rest of the Easterners simply stood around on the floor, not understanding about the rats — till the clinking of dishes brought the brutes out in their hordes. That clinking seemed like a signal to them. It seemed to mean, "Come to the cook-house door, boys!"

7 — It was then that the Easterners discovered what all those metal rings on ropes were for. The idea was to grab them and swing yourself clear of the floor to avoid being eaten alive! What a scramble there was! Danny scrambled with the rest. And the rats scrambled too — for anything that could be eaten. Longlegs swung on a pair of rings, and Tarbrush, the dwarf drummer, swarmed up on the giant boy's knee. Danny noticed that the wee fellow had a queer Eastern flute with him.

8 — "That's one of those magic flutes you Easterners use to charm snakes, isn't it?" exclaimed Longlegs. Tarbrush nodded, and Danny ordered him to play. "Maybe its magic notes will charm rats too." So the wee chap tootled a queer Eastern tune, and to Danny's delight he saw the nibbling rats prick up their ears and turn towards the sound. "Keep on playing!" cried the ten-foot boy. He tucked the tootling fluter between his legs and swung towards the next ring.

9 — Entranced by the music, the rats followed the fluter. Danny went swinging on, and won the race out of the hall, across the courtyard and on to the drawbridge, carrying Tarbrush in one giant hand. Fortunately the drawbridge was partly raised, and with the dwarf still tootling away Danny leapt clean over the moat. It was a colossal leap. No-one with legs less than about a couple of yards long could have made it.

10 — Tarbrush tootled on his magic flute and Danny chortled as the music-mad rats poured over the drawbridge. The strange lilt of the music acted like a magnet, drawing them out from their holes in every nook and corner of the castle to come tumbling into the waters of the moat. And that was the end of them. Tarbrush piped till he was purple in the face, but at last the rush stopped. There wasn't a squeak to be heard.

11 — Sir Toby was overjoyed to be free of the pests at last. "What a Christmas present for Rathole Towers!" he cried. "We'll be able to come down to earth again and live like men instead of birds. Danny, you and the Prince must share my Christmas feast." And so there was a wonderful celebration in the Rathole hall. Only one rat appeared when the dishes clanked — and that one was a stupid beast which had crawled inside a cracker and came out with a bang when the cracker was pulled! But the feast went on very happily, even though the elephant stole a pudding by making a trunk call through a window, and a camel snaffled the holly decorations. That didn't worry Danny. He tucked up his cuff and stuffed himself with duff. So a great time was had by all, and Longlegs even forgot he was a prisoner — till next morning!

Sammy Shrinko

Every picture tells a story~ and the ones on these pages are no exception! These pages show some of the Beano's less well-known characters from the early years. Less well-known, maybe, but they can still raise plenty of Beano-sized Christmas cackles!

Have-a-go-Joe

Little Nell and Peter Pell

The Magic Lollipops

Maxi's Taxi

Rip Van Wink (He's 700 years old)

More than fifty years ago, The Dandy's centre pages were full of
quick-fire Christmas chuckles from characters like
Freddy the Fearless Fly, Hair-Oil Hal and Meddlesome Matty.

FREDDY THE FEARLESS FLY

HAIR-OIL HAL YOUR BARBER PAL

MEDDLESOME MATTY

CHRISTMAS Feasts come in all shapes and sizes, just like the folk from the pages of The Dandy and The Beano. Each story is hilarious — there's not a "turkey" or a "duff" one in this whole section!

BANG!

GINGER'S SUPER JEEP

Ginger Griffiths is a lucky lad. He has a marvellous soap-box cart which can travel at tremendous speed and can even climb walls. A few weeks ago Ginger joined Syd Sharp's Circus. He was a great hit, but some of the other stars were jealous of Ginger's success.

To the youngsters' amazement, Ginger drove his Super Jeep right up the end wall.

IT was Christmas Day and Syd Sharp was putting on a show for the children in a nearby hospital. Holding a banner aloft, Ginger Griffiths, in his Super Jeep, led the circus procession into the ward.

And then upside down back along the ceiling. Here he fixed the banner amongst the decorations.

That done, he drove to the centre of the ceiling, untied a knot, and a trapeze dropped from the Jeep.

The next part of the stunt strained the holding power of the Jeep's wonder wheels to the utmost—for Crumpet, the clown, swung from the trapeze.

The youngsters grinned in delight. It was a wonderful show. But there was one sour-faced gent who didn't think so. He was Slim Swales, the masked trick-rider.

Suddenly a garden rake shot through an open window near the Christmas tree. Hidden hands buried the prongs in the branches.

A quick tug and the tree fell —right on top of Syd Sharp.

It was a dirty trick—and a dangerous one! The burning candles set the branches alight. Smoke belched through the ward.

Oblivious to his own danger, Syd pluckily tried to push the blazing tree out through the window.

But it was too big. It stuck and nothing would budge it.

Ginger shot into action. The doorway was packed with panic-stricken children so he zoomed across the ceiling and out through the top of the door—still upside down.

Outside he hunted around in the gardener's shed until he found a hook and rope. Then he threw the hook into the blazing tree.

The terrific power of the Jeep did the trick. Ginger put it into reverse and it yanked the tree outside in a twinkling. The danger was over.

Syd Sharp was able to get his burns and bruises treated on the spot, and the nurses started clearing up the mess, for everyone was determined that the show must go on.

ut it wasn't all plain sailing. anta Claus failed to appear at he appointed time, so Syd sent Ginger away to look for him.

Ginger shot off through the snow in his Super Jeep and soon found the cause of the delay. The circus lorry with Santa aboard had skidded into a ditch.

The lorry was badly damaged and there was no hope of it delivering the toys. But Ginger had an idea. He explained his plan to Santa Claus. At once they took Santa's sledge off the lorry and piled all the toys on to it.

Then Ginger harnessed the sledge to the Super Jeep and set off for the hospital.

Just outside the gates he unhitched the Jeep and the "reindeer" took over. And what a comical-looking creature it was!

The kids in the hospital certainly got a big laugh when it pranced up the drive, trying to catch the pie Santa was dangling in front of its nose.

o, thanks to Ginger and his Super Jeep, all the oung patients got their presents from Santa. And hat with the eats, reindeer rides, and ices, they all agreed it was a smashing Christmas party.

MERRY CHRISTMAS

ICES

HAIRY DAN

This bearded figure isn't Santa Claus — his whiskers are much longer! Hairy Dan appeared in the Beano from issue one in 1938 right through to late 1946, also guesting in most of the Beano Books of the 1940s.

Old Hairy Dan, one snowy day,
Meets two young scamps who bar his way
By throwing snowballs in his track,
And knocking Dan flat on his back.

Now Dan is very mad indeed,
'Cause he was going to have a feed
Of Christmas fare, which, sad to say,
The boys pinched and then ran away.

But Dan is wise, as you well know,
And says, " By this short cut I'll go."
Now what's he up to, do you think?
Just watch him give that sly old wink !

Now at their house old Danny spies
The two young lads lay down their prize
Upon a table close beside
A window which is open wide.

Then off the little fellows run
For knives and forks. They shout, " What fun!"
But little do these youngsters know
The pudding is about to go.

Unknown to them, they'd placed the food
On Dan's long beard, and so the pud-
Ding's neatly hauled back by our friend,
Who, as you see, wins in the end !

8

KORKY THE CAT

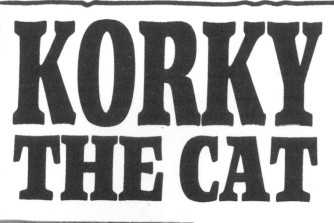

Despite the austerity of the wartime years the Dandy could be relied on to give their readers plenty of laughs at the expense of certain villains of the day, such as Hitler and Goering. The Dandy's "Addie and Hermy" were portrayed trying to conquer hunger rather than Hungary, and turkey rather than Turkey at Christmastime!

LORD SNOOTY
And His Pals

COLONEL Crackpot's Circus

Ho! Ho! Ho! Looks like poor Santa Claus couldn't keep up with the Beano's Billy Whizz this Christmas! Or maybe he's over-eaten too!

LOOK AT COLONEL GRUMBLY WORKING IN THAT DINGY OFFICE. LET'S LURE HIM OUT AND BRIGHTEN THE PLACE UP WITH SOME CHRISTMAS DECORATIONS.

CORPORAL CLOTT

HULLO, IS THAT YOU, COLONEL GRUMBLY, SIR? THERE'S SOMEONE LOCKED IN THE CLOTHING STORE. COULD YOU COME AT ONCE?

OH, ALL RIGHT!

BAH! NOTHING BUT INTERRUPTIONS.

NO SIGN OF THE KEY. HEY, CLOTT! BRING THAT TREE OVER HERE.

CHARGE! THAT'S IDEA, MEN! WE'LL BURST OPEN THE DOOR.

BAH! ANOTHER INTERRUPTION! I'LL HAVE TO CHECK THE MAIN SWITCH.

OH, DEAR, MY MATCH HAS GONE OUT! YAHOO! WHAT'S THAT?

OOPS! I'VE BUMPED INTO SOMEONE.

AHA! I FELL AGAINST A BUSH OR SOMETHING. IT WILL DO AS A FLARE.

SUFFERING SERGEANT! THERE GOES MY SECOND TREE UP IN SMOKE.

WE'VE GOT IN AT LAST. WE DON'T HAVE A REAL TREE NOW, BUT I'LL GLUE THESE SHEETS OF PAPER TOGETHER AND MAKE A PAPER ONE.

WHAT'S BEEN GOING ON, CLOTT?

WE'VE BEEN HANGING CHRISTMAS DECORATIONS ROUND YOUR OFFICE, SIR!

BUT THESE PAPERS ARE THE ORDERS I RECEIVED FROM GENERAL CHINSTRAP! THEY GAVE DETAILS OF THE EXERCISE TO BE HELD DURING CHRISTMAS WEEK. NOW THEY'VE BEEN CUT TO BITS!

Party Invitation

Poor Biffo! In this bear-y story from 1940, he just couldn't BEAR being left out of the party, so he . . . oh, go on — we invite you to read it yourself!

The council of the escapers was held in Creepy's own classroom— with Creepy standing right there!

Creepy should have smelled a rat—but he didn't.

What Creepy didn't know was that Winker had previously stuck the bottle to the door with chewing gum.

It was the door of Creepy's own study that Winker was unscrewing. What on earth for? Winker wasn't telling. Not yet, anyway.

The mystery was deepening. What could the wangler want with a huge chunk off the goalposts?

Only Winker could have thought of it—a home-made snowplough to open up an escape route! But there was still the question of food supplies.

Winker laid the bait to trap a little rat.

Yes! Wallie had swallowed the bait!

So Wallie lost the grub he had swiped from the chaps who had swiped it!

Wallie nearly swallowed his back teeth when he saw that his big brother was leading the whole Third Form in a break-out to get home for Christmas.

One flying dive and the mop-headed Watson had joined his elders and betters in the Escapers' Club.

It just showed how deep the snow was. It had taken the boys hours to get here—and they were still inside the school grounds!

There was lots of firewood—things like cricket stumps, bats and benches.
Some sacrifices had to be made to get home for Christmas.

MEANWHILE, BACK IN THE SCHOOL ~~

IT'S UNCANNY, CREEP, BUT I CAN'T FIND A SINGLE THIRD FORM BOY ANYWHERE IN THE BUILDING! OUT YOU GO AND SEARCH THE GROUNDS!

OH DEAR! IF YOU INSIST, HEADMASTER!

Poor old Creepy! He always got the dirty work to do.

ONE HOUR LATER ~

BAH! THE TELEPHONE'S STILL DEAD! ..... AH. YOU'VE RETURNED, CREEP! DID YOU FIND THE BOYS?

G-GASP! N-NO, SIR, AND IT'S TERRIBLE OUT THERE! SNOWING HARD! ALL THE LITTLE PERISHERS HAVE MAYBE PERISHED IN THE SNOW.

Creepy crept back thankfully. He felt that nothing could live out there in the blizzard.

NEXT MORNING ~~

COME ON, LADS, LET'S DIG THE CAR OUT AND BE ON OUR WAY!

The escapers had had a feed and a sleep while Creepy was still thawing out.

GOSH, THE SNOW MAKES EVERYTHING LOOK DIFFERENT.... ANYBODY KNOW WHICH WAY THE GATE IS?

LEFT!

RIGHT!

STRAIGHT ON!

It seemed there were three possible ways to the school gate. Which to take?

This must have been the wrong way —but there was no stopping now.

OOPS! WATCH IT, WINKER! YOU'VE MISSED THE GATE! AND THIS IS WHERE THE ROAD BENDS! LOOK OUT!

OO-ER! WE'VE GONE THROUGH THE FENCE!

CRASH!

The snowplough suddenly seemed to take wings! It shot through the fence on the top of the bank above the canal, carrying before it an avalanche of snow, and trailing behind it a wailing tail of boys on skis and sleds and sitting in boxes! Creepy's old boneshaker was going to shake up a few young bones in a split second from now.

Wonder of wonders! The ice was very thick. It didn't break —and no bones were broken either. What's more, the canal made a perfect highway for the Escapers' Club.

The trains were running —and so were the Third Formers!

There was just one job for the master wangler to do—send a radio message of courage and good cheer to the marooned masters.

....AND HERE IS A SPECIAL REQUEST BY THE BOYS OF FORM THREE AT GREYTOWERS SCHOOL FOR A RECORD FOR THE HEADMASTER AND THEIR FORM MASTER MR CREEP .... HERE IT IS .... "GOD REST YE, MERRY GENTLEMEN, LET NOTHING YOU DISMAY"

The Watson brothers shared a giant half of a colossal turkey for their daring.

Mr Creep had the smaller share of a charred sausage! But only the brave deserve the fare!

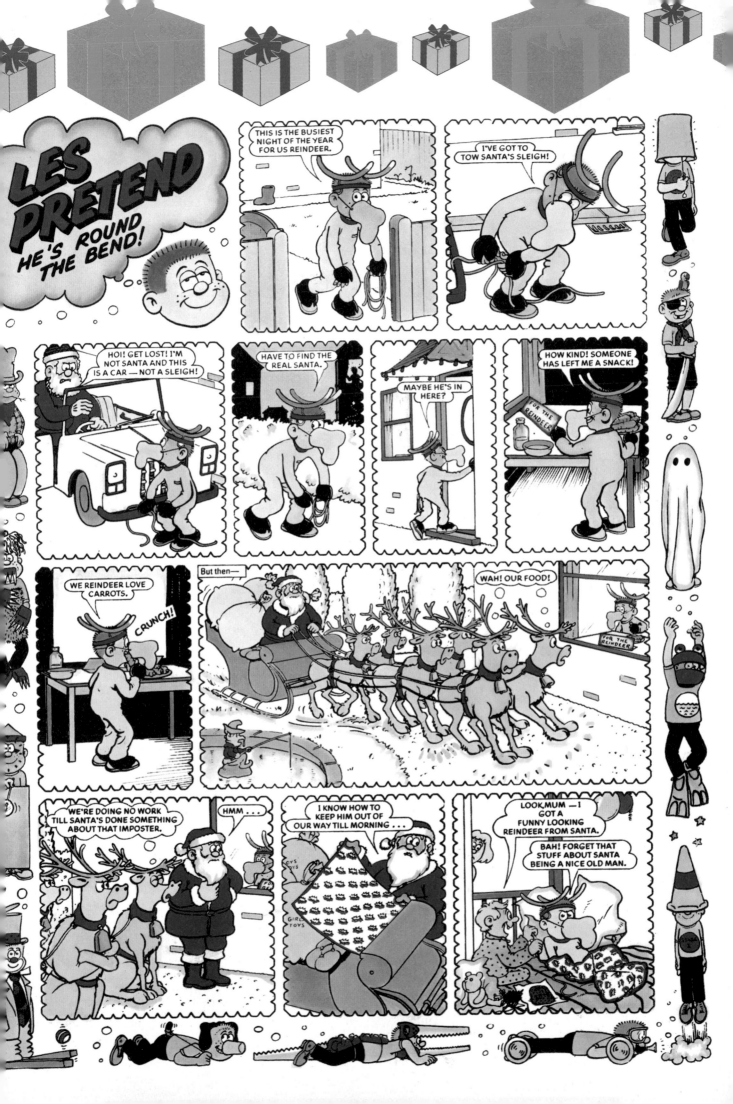

BRINGING UP DENNIS!

TOLD FOR THE FIRST TIME

ADVENTURES THAT HAPPENED YEARS AGO WHEN DENNIS WAS EIGHTEEN MONTHS OR SO

Here's the Dandy-est dawg in the whole dog-gone book! Yup! From The Dandy 1973, it's . . .

DESPERATE DAWG

Sledge-pulling, present-giving, party games — yes, even the Dandy Wonder-Dog enjoys Christmas, as you can see from these pictures taken from the Black Bob books of the 1950s!

BOLD BOB, The Bandit-Buster

IT was Christmas Day, but Black Bob and his master were hard at work as usual. It wasn't a holiday for them. There had been a fall of snow during the night making it difficult for the sheep to find grass to eat, so the shepherd and his dog had to feed them with turnips. First Glenn loaded a cart with turnips, then while Black Bob led the horse down the field by the reins, Andrew Glenn stood in the cart and forked out the turnips to the hungry sheep.

2 — There were hundreds of sheep to be fed in the fields round the farm and Bob and Glenn were kept busy until well on in the afternoon. When all the sheep had been attended to the shepherd and his dog hurried home, for there was another important job to be done that day — Andrew Glenn was to be Santa Claus at a children's party in the village. So the shepherd dressed himself up in a big red cloak, then he brushed and combed his clever collie.

3 — Glenn wanted Bob to be looking his best, for the collie had a part to play, too. It was Bob's job to pull the sledge laden with Christmas presents. Soon they were both ready and they set off for the village with Bob harnessed to the sledge. And how the children laughed and cheered when Santa Claus arrived at the hall with his sledge-load of presents. Bob helped to hand out the gifts to the youngsters, then everyone sat down to a real Christmas tuck-in.

4 — When the feed was over, the children started to play musical chairs. They got Black Bob to join in and soon the collie was having great fun. Bob had played musical chairs before and he knew he was supposed to leap on to a chair when the music stopped. Being much quicker and nimbler on his feet than the children, Bob was usually first to reach a chair, and in the end he won the game. But the children didn't mind. They cheered loudly.

BLACK BOB The Dandy ~~wonder~~ dog Christmas

PRINCE WHOOPEE

Your princely pal is a perfect pest who performs a profusion of pranks in the palace!

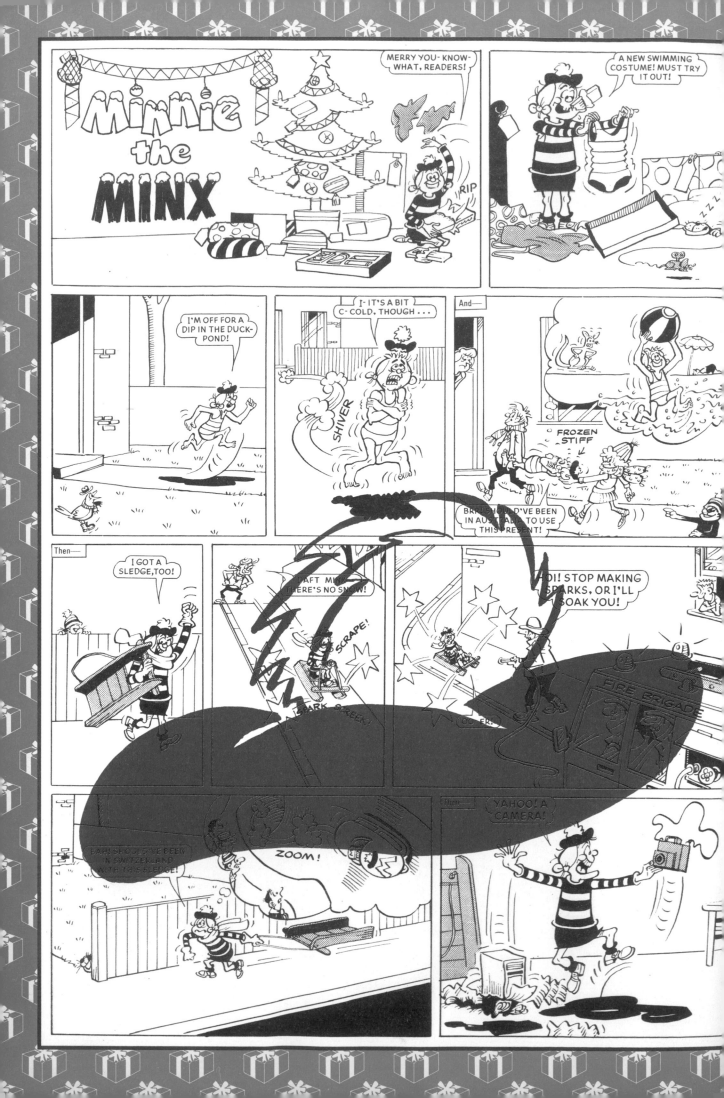

PUP PARADE

STARRING the BASH STREET DOGS

Merry Christmas, pups— H-HEY! Where are they?

EDITOR'S VOICE

Oh, there you are ~ out you come and say "Merry Christmas" to the readers!

No! We're not moving!

Why not?

Because we remember what happened last year— THAT'S WHY NOT!

LAST YEAR~

Jingle bells~ Jingle bells...

YULE LOG

THEN—

MERRY CHRISTMAS, PUPS~ HOW DO YOU LIKE THE SLEDGE WE GOT FROM SANTA?

ZIP!

YAH! PESKY ROAD HOG! BOO!

WHERE'S MY SPECS?

THEN—

GURK!

KAFLUMPFF!

WE GOT BOWS AND ARROWS FROM SANTA!

We noticed!

Aw! Won't you come out and wish the readers "Merry Christmas"?

NO! WE ALWAYS GET HURT OUT THERE AT CHRISTMAS! WE'RE PLAYING SAFE!

THEN—

WHEE!

BANG!

THUMP!

OW!

AGH!

YARGH! It's even MORE dangerous inside!

Anyway now you're out, you can wish the readers a "Merry Christmas," can't you?

Oh, very well!

MERRY GRRRISTMAS!

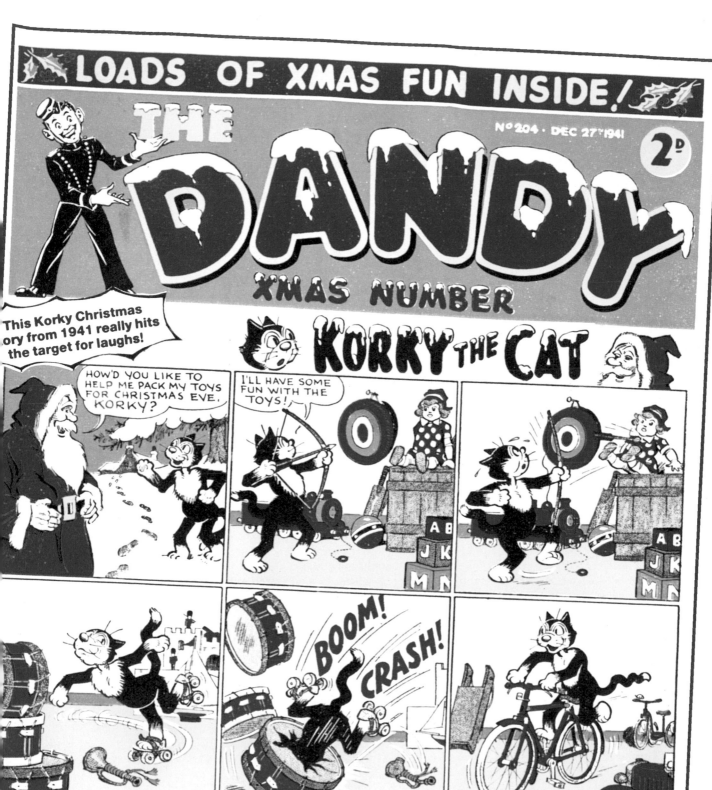

LOADS OF XMAS FUN INSIDE!

THE **DANDY**

XMAS NUMBER

Nº 204 · DEC 27th 1941

2d

This Korky Christmas story from 1941 really hits the target for laughs!

KORKY the CAT

A PRESENT TO SOOTY FROM THE ALLEY KIDS

Sooty's Christmas Gift.

ON Christmas morning, Sooty Solomon's store at the corner of Muffin Alley was closed like all the other shops in the district. But soon after breakfast the door was unlocked by Susan Wallace, who ran the shop for the clever cat, and Sooty stepped out daintily into the Alley.

It was a grand morning. As yet, none of the Alley kids had come out, and Muffin Alley was deserted. Sooty stood on the bottom step of his shop and looked around with interest. He was the only cat in the world who owned a shop, his old mistress having left it to him when she died.

Now, as Sooty turned to look at his shop, he saw, for the first time, a Christmas stocking tied to the door handle. He had walked past it on his way out without noticing it.

Sooty was puzzled as he reached up and unhooked it with his paw.

It was quite a small stocking, with a label tied to the top.

"A present to Sooty," this said, "from the Alley kids."

Suddenly, Sooty stiffened and arched his back, for inside the stocking he had just seen a mouse — quite a large mouse! His whiskers bristled and his paw rose to strike, then he saw that it was only a toy mouse, a clockwork mouse made of tin, and cleverly painted to look like a real, live mouse!

Using his paws and nose, Sooty turned the stocking upside down and the mouse rolled out. As it sat in the street, it looked every inch a real mouse.

Sooty pranced playfully around the toy, and stabbed at it with his paw. There was a whirring noise, and the mouse darted away at top speed. The kiddies had left it already wound up, so that Sooty could play with it.

The big black cat was delighted. Leaping after the speeding mouse, he was in time to give it a pat before it ran into the wall. The mouse swung in the opposite direction and headed back for the steps.

To and fro on the pavement before the shop ran the clockwork mouse, with Sooty leaping after it. The black cat was so busy enjoying himself that he did not notice danger approaching!

Not until he heard a sudden snarl did Sooty realise there was anything wrong. He had been so busy with his Christmas present, that he had not noticed a rough-haired terrier creeping up on him! The dog's teeth snapped in mid-air as Sooty made a desperate leap for the window-sill.

His back arched, and, spitting angrily, Sooty Solomon turned round, but the terrier, having missed the cat, made a dive at the toy mouse and seized it in his teeth. The wheels whirled around, and Sooty feared that the dog would break his toy.

Determined to save his Christmas gift, the angry cat leaped down and landed on the terrier's back.

As Sooty landed, he sank his claws in the terrier's thick skin. The dog gave a loud howl of surprise, and bounded into the street. Sooty hung on, hissing and spitting, while the terrier, dropping the toy mouse, whirled round and round, trying to snap at the clinging cat.

Suddenly, half crazy with fear, the dog started to run, hoping to shake Sooty Solomon from his back. At that moment, a little girl stepped out of a doorway just down the Alley. She was holding a large enamelled jug.

As the terrier bounded towards her, the frightened girl jumped back dropping the jug. To Sooty's great delight, the jug dropped neatly over the dog's head!

The black cat jumped off smartly and watched the frightened terrier careering around with its head inside the jug.

Howling loudly, the puzzled dog fled down the Alley.

Sooty Solomon, delighted with his adventure, followed to see the fun.

Stampede!

AS the fleeing dog approached the main street at the end of Muffin Alley, Sooty heard the sound of music. A big procession, led by a brass band, was coming down the centre of the street.

A circus had come to Sooty's town and the performers were holding their parade, led by the brass band. Just behind the band plodded a huge elephant, with flapping ears and long swinging trunk.

Into the middle of the procession burst the terrier, with the jug still firmly fixed on its head.

Clank-clank! The jug rattled on the roadway as the dog shook its head. Its muffled howling added to the din. Right beneath the feet of the elephant whirled the blinded, terrified dog, and the huge tusker came to a sudden stop. Its big ears flattened back and it reared high on its hind legs, trumpeting loudly in terror.

Then, badly scared, the elephant burst from its place in the procession.

"Stop, Rajah, stop!" shouted its Indian keeper, who had been walking on the pavement, but before he could grasp the elephant's rope halter, the huge animal bolted.

Next moment, to Sooty's horror, the elephant turned into Muffin Alley!

Sooty knew that the Alley kids would be running out at the sound of the music, and would be caught in the path

he mighty elephant. There was great
ger that some of them would be
mpled by the frightened tusker
ess it could be stopped.

he black cat went into action even as
hought of this, for he had an idea.
ooty Solomon bounded up the Alley
 a black streak. He passed the
mpeding elephant, and reached the
s of his shop with a few seconds to
re.

 little farther down the Alley, more
 a dozen boys and girls were
nding in the elephant's path,
ified, panic-stricken, hardly able to
e. The elephant, thudding down the
re of the street, was almost on top
em when Sooty sprang his surprise.

he clockwork mouse had fallen
nst the step where the terrier had
pped it. Sooty swiftly picked it up in
eeth and placed it the right way up.
gave it a pat with his paw, and, to his
 the clockwork started to whirr. Out
 the street in the path of Rajah's
, the huge tusker stopped so
denly that it sat down on its tail.

errified squeals came from the
hant as the toy mouse ran past in
t of the beast's huge feet and hit the
 on the other side of the Alley. The
se spun about and began to recross
Alley.

ajah rose to his feet, turned, and
pared to flee in the opposite
ction, but at that moment his
per arrived, out of breath, and,
bing the elephant by the halter,
an to soothe it with kind words and
le strokes.

ery soon, under the Indian's expert
ntions, the huge beast calmed
n.

he children edged forward to look at
great creature which could be both
ierce and so gentle. One of the boys
e it a bun, and the last of the tusker's
s fled.

I hate to think what would have
pened if something had not stopped
ah from stampeding down the
ey," said the circus boss, who had
 up. "These kids have had a narrow
ape. It seems to me that the only way
nake it up to them is to give them a
 on the elephant. Come along,
ies, and have a free ride!"

o, while Sooty Solomon sat on the
 outside his shop, with the toy
se silent and still beside him, the
dren whooped and shrieked with
ght as the elephant carried them up
down the Alley.

ooty knew that it was the kids'
istmas gift that had saved the day. It
ked like being a Happy Christmas
r all!

RAGGY MUFFIN
THE DANDY DOG

KORKY'S CHRISTMAS GREETING.

" Dandy " readers, listen hard
To Korky's Christmas greeting.
He hopes you'll have a right
good time,
With plenty Christmas eating.

A MERRY CHRISTMAS, ALL!

Yum-yum-yum! This plum-duff's
good,
I hope yours is as swell.
I hope your stocking's brimming
o'er
With toys and sweets, as well!

I hope that you'll get frost and
slides,
I hope that snow will fall.
And, last, I hope that you will
have

A MERRY CHRISTMAS, ALL!

Korky's Christmas Greeting

Hip, hurray! See what I've
got.
Just look what good old Santa's
brought—
A great big fish, a perfect
winner.
Yum, yum, it's for my Christmas
dinner!
I hope your stockings, girls and
boys,
Are just as full with sweets and
toys.
I hope you get plum-duff and
cake;
I hope you don't get tummy-
ache!
I hope you get a Christmas tree.
A party—even two or three.
I wish you lots and lots of fun.
A MERRY CHRISTMAS
EVERYONE!

In the Dandy's early years
Korky usually appears
On a different page at Christmas time
With Xmas greetings, all in rhyme.
The Beano's had some poems too—
Here's one from 1988 for you!

KORKY'S CHRISTMAS
GREETING.

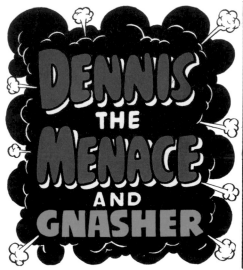

Roger's "stocking up" on dodges with this page from The Beano in 1969.

IVY the TERRIBLE

E Your Pal From The Palace

APRIL FOOLS' DAY

Nº 70 · APR. 1ᵗ · 1939
EVERY FRIDAY

THE DANDY COMIC

KORKY THE CAT

COME ALONG WITH KORKY!
HE'S GOING TO THE ZOO!
HE'S GOING TO GET A BIG SURPRISE
AND SO, WE THINK, ARE YOU!

DESPERATE DAN

DESPERATE DAN

DESPERATE DAN

Dennis the MENACE

NO WONDER POOR OLD EGGO GRIEVES
HE'S SWEEP-SWEEP-SWEEPING UP THE LEAVES

BUT SUDDENLY HE HAS A WHEEZE
AND PUTS THEM ALL BACK ON THE TREES!

THE BEANO COMIC

No. 321—NOV. 1st, 1947

2D

Beano's Wonder Boy from nearly 40 years ago wondered what it would be like to be Santa Claus. Now you can wonder who these Santas are! All will be revealed as you read this next section.

BULLY BEEF AND CHIPS

MAY I HAVE A FEW OF MY PALS IN FOR A LITTLE PARTY? WE CAN PLAY WITH EACH OTHERS' CHRISTMAS PRESENTS, MUM.

OF COURSE, CHIPS.

THANKS, MUM! I'LL GO AND INVITE MY PALS NOW.

HELLO, CHIPS! YOU'LL ASK ME TO YOUR PARTY, WON'T YOU?

LET GO, BEEFY!

GRAB!

YOU WILL INVITE ME, WON'T YOU?

ER—OKAY! SO LONG AS YOU DON'T SMASH THINGS UP!

SHAKE!

GURR! ME? SMASH THINGS UP? I'LL SMASH YOU FOR SAYING THAT!

OOYAH!

BONK!

HO! HO! SEE YOU LATER!

NO, YOU WON'T, BECAUSE YOU'RE NOT GETTING TO COME NOW!

IN THE ATTIC

SO CHIPS WON'T LET ME IN? WE'LL SEE ABOUT THAT!

LATER—AT THE PARTY—

CHOO-CHOO-CHOO— HELLO, HERE'S SOMEONE ELSE COMING TO JOIN THE PARTY.

WOW! IT'S BEEFY! I'D KNOW THAT VOICE ANY-WHERE.

HO-HO! MERRY CHRISTMAS, KIDS!

THAT'S RIGHT—AND I DIDN'T COME DOWN THE CHIMNEY EITHER. I SNEAKED IN A WINDOW!

PLAYING AT TRAINS, LADS? GOOD! THAT MAKES MY JOB A LOT EASIER.

WOW! OW!

OUCH!

THUMP!

AARGH!

GROAN!

I'VE COME TO TAKE ALL YOUR NEW TOYS! THAT'S FOR NOT LETTING ME IN TO YOUR PARTY.

THIS'LL HELP ME TEACH HIM A LESSON!

ER, WHY DON'T YOU HAVE A SEAT, BEEFY? THE GRUB WILL BE ALONG IN A MINUTE!

GRUB? GOOD!

OKAY! BUT NO TRICKS!

ME, PLAY TRICKS? NEVER!

YEOWWCH!

HO-HO! I THINK BEEFY GOT THE POINT!

FLAP!

PRANG!

HELP! I CAN'T SEE!

HERE'S SOME CAKES AND LEMONADE, BOYS!

EEK!

CRASH!

OOYAH!

HO-HO! BEEFY'S A RED-NOSED SANTA! WONDER IF HE'S GOT A RED-NOSED REINDEER TO MATCH?

GURR! GET OUT, YOU YOUNG WRECKER!

DONG!

OOYAH! OUCH!

JIMMY AND HIS MAGIC PATCH

1 — Whistling merrily Jimmy Watson tramped along in the snow. There were not many more days to pass before Christmas. A gaily decorated shop window caught his eye and he stopped to read the placard inside. "Well, young man," asked a cheery, elderly gent, "and what is Santa Claus bringing you?" Jimmy waved a derisive hand. "Huh!" he replied, "there's no such person."

2 — No sooner had the words left his lips than — swoosh! The magic patch on his pants carried him through space once more. The next second Jimmy was standing before a lonely building in the midst of towering snow-clad mountains. It was the sign at the opening to a flight of steps that Jimmy stared at, however. "Toyland," he muttered in amazement. "Well, now that I'm here I'd better take a look inside."

3 — Cautiously he tiptoed up the stairs into a well-lit passage. An even brighter light came from the end, and Jimmy made towards it. When he reached it and peeped inside the surprised lad nearly fainted — and no small wonder! The cavern at which he looked was stacked with the most numerous and assorted toys that Jimmy had ever seen. He stepped over to a pile of boxing gloves that caught his eye.

"Gosh," he murmured to himself as he tried on a pair. "I've always wanted a pair of these." He turned and looked for something to punch and saw just the very thing! A leather punch-ball stood only a couple of yards away. "Oh, boy," the lad chuckled gleefully. "Now for some fun." He stepped towards the punch-ball so excited that he failed to notice the trap-door until it was too late.

4 — He stepped on the wooden boards in front of the punch-ball. Immediately the door gave way on well-oiled hinges. A gasp escaped Jimmy. It was pitch black below, and he shut his eyes as he felt himself dropping. He found himself on a well-polished shute and slid down and down until he thought it would never end. Suddenly it did, however, and Jimmy was shot out into a well-lit room.

5 — It was a workshop and seven little dwarfs were making toys of all descriptions. Their amazement was obvious as they gazed at Jimmy, who was still too dazed to do anything but sit and blink at the gnome-like figures. But he wasn't allowed to sit long. Suddenly the dwarfs threw down their tools. "We'll teach him to sneak in here," one of them roared. "Come on, let's get him."

— Suddenly the dwarfs were upon Jimmy. It seemed to him the ... men were all over him at once. He was helpless among so many ... y bodies, and soon his hands were securely tied behind his back. ... cap, which had been knocked off in the scrimmage, was banged on ... head and he was forced to his feet. A prod with a saw helped him ... as he was marched out of the room.

7 — Up and down stairs and along stone passages he was led by the seven very business-like dwarfs. At length the party stopped before a large studded door with a brass nameplate on it marked "Santa Claus, Esq." A dwarf knocked smartly on the door. There was no answer. He knocked again. Still no answer. "Something fishy here," the dwarf muttered. The little man pushed open the door.

— The sight that met their eyes shocked everyone in the doorway. ... ta Claus himself crouched on the floor, bound hand and foot. ... nding over him, sword in hand, was a masked figure. In his left ... d he held a bag of money, taken from the open safe. "Try to ... erfere any of you, and Santa here will suffer," the rogue said. "You ... nd still." But Jimmy didn't mean to let the robber off with this.

9 — He noticed a football on the floor in front of him, and an idea flashed into his mind. In one quick movement, so fast that it was practically all over before anybody thought about trying to stop him, the lad drew back his foot and let drive at the football. Wham! A professional would have envied that kick. It soared from Jimmy's toe and landed full force on the robber's ugly, masked face.

... — The rogue dropped his sword with the shock. That was where ... dwarfs did a quick bit of work. They piled on the robber and dealt ... h him as they had dealt with Jimmy. Soon he too, was helpless, and ... dwarfs freed Santa Claus. The first thing that genial old gentleman ... was to pat Jimmy's shoulder for saving his money. "There'll be ... re Christmas presents for the children, thanks to you," he said.

11 — The praise was short-lived, however. Suddenly Jimmy found himself back in modern times once more. That night he went to bed with his queer adventure still in his mind. He lay awake a long time thinking about it. That was how he managed to see, out of the corner of his eye, his father in red cloak and beard, bring in presents. Little did his father know how near Jimmy had been to the real Santa Claus!

DESPERATE DAN

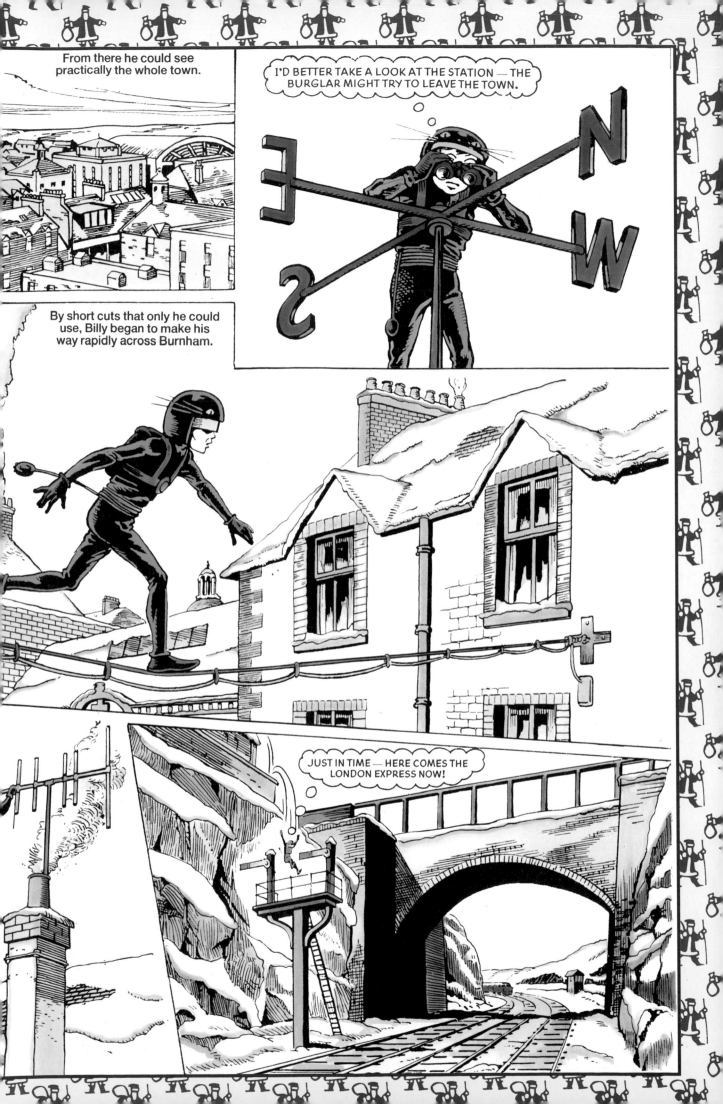

JAMMY MR SAMMY

WINKER WATSON

CHRISTMAS time was fast approaching, and Winker Watson and his pals at Greytowers School were looking forward to getting off home for the holidays. But before then, there was another event to look forward to, the end-of-term Christmas party.

CREEPY'S GIVEN US THE MONEY TO BUY A CHRISTMAS TREE FOR THE PARTY, TROTTY, SO LET'S GET CRACKING!

Winker was the world's top schoolboy wangler, and as he passed the gates of the cop college next door to Greytowers, he saw a sight that set his wily brain racing.

HEY, LOOK, TROTTY! IF WE COULD GET HOLD OF ONE OF THOSE, WE COULD SPEND THE TREE MONEY ON EXTRA GRUB FOR THE PARTY!

POLICE COLLEGE

But the Superintendent of the cop college must have been a mind reader. No sooner had Winker stepped inside the gates than the Super appeared, scowling.

HEY, IF YOU'RE THINKING OF PINCHING ONE OF MY TREES FOR CHRISTMAS, YOUNG WATSON, YOU CAN FORGET IT! BE OFF WITH YOU AT ONCE!

But Winker didn't give up easily. He soon thought up a plan that would make the Super uproot one of his own trees!

I'LL TIE ONE END OF THIS ROPE ON TO A TREE, TROTTY, AND YOU TIE YOUR END ON TO THE BACK BUMPER OF THE SUPER'S CAR—THEN WHEN HE DRIVES OFF HE'LL PULL IT OUT OF THE GROUND FOR US.

The Super stepped into his car without noticing the rope. He drove off—and Winker's plan began to work.

TOOT-TOOT!

THERE HE GOES, WINKER, AND OUT COMES THE TREE—NOW WHAT?

WHEN THE TREE HITS THE GATE THE ROPE WILL SNAP!

But that rope was a lot stronger than Winker thought! It was the cop college gates that gave way under the impact. What a clatter!

CLANK!
CRASH!

POLICE

I DON'T TRUST HIM, TROTTY! LET'S LEAVE IT AND COME BACK AFTER DARK.

The Superintendent was furious. And he didn't need much detective skill to decide who must be to blame.

GURR! I BET THOSE BOYS ARE RESPONSIBLE FOR THIS! I'LL USE THE TREE TO SET A TRAP FOR THEM IF THEY TRY IT AGAIN!

Winker thought that must be the end of his tree-pinching plan. Imagine his surprise when he saw the uprooted tree, unattended, just waiting to be grabbed.

FANCY THE SUPER GOING OFF AND LEAVING THE TREE LIKE THAT FOR US TO TAKE, WINKER!

I DON'T TRUST HIM, TROTTY! LET'S LEAVE IT AND COME BACK AFTER DARK.

en he was sure the coast was ar, Winker found he was right to be suspicious.

COME AND LOOK AT THIS, TROTTY! THAT SNEAKY SUPERINTENDENT HAS SET TRAP TO DRENCH ANYONE TOUCHING THE TREE!

But Winker was pretty good at setting booby traps himself. He dismantled this one and began to rearrange it.

I'VE UNTIED THE ROPE AND I'LL MAKE IT INTO A TRIP ROPE WHILE YOU TAKE THE TREE BACK TO SCHOOL.

Back at Greytowers, Winker gathered a few things he would need for the next part of his wangle. Creepy's old cap and gown, for a start.

A little later, the Super was patrolling his plantation when he spotted a shadowy figure snooping around.

WELL, I NEVER! THAT FELLOW CREEP IS AFTER ONE OF MY TREES NOW!

HEY, YOU!

The Super yelled and chased after Creepy. But of course it wasn't Creepy at all. It was Winker Watson!

ker led the Super a merry chase d finally got the bobby caught by his own booby trap!

OOYAH!

SPLASH!

The Super was red with rage—and with red paint as well. He stormed round to Greytowers. But his story sounded so ridiculous to Creepy that the master only laughed.

DON'T BE SILLY, SUPERINTENDENT! OF COURSE OUR CHRISTMAS TREE ISN'T ONE OF YOURS. COME AND SEE FOR YOURSELF!

By this time, the Super's tree had had its roots sawn off and was glittering with tinsel and lights. He couldn't identify it.

GURR! THEY ALL LOOK THE SAME WHEN THEY'RE DECORATED, MR CREEP!

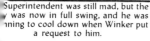

Superintendent was still mad, but the y was now in full swing, and he was nning to cool down when Winker put a request to him.

W THAT YOU'VE HAD A CUP OF TEA AND SOME GOODIES, SUPERINTENDENT, I WONDER IF YOU WOULD DO US A FAVOUR?

The Super's red-painted uniform made a great Santa suit, and Winker soon shaped a beard for him out of a mass of cotton wool. At last he saw the funny side of his night's adventure—and Winker made sure there was a box of cigars for him after he'd handed out everyone else's presents!

WITH MY WELLINGTON BOOTS AND MY RED NIGHTCAP, WATSON, I THINK THE SUPER MAKES A SMASHING SANTA CLAUS, DON'T YOU?

NOT HALF, MR CREEP, BUT I STILL THINK HE SHOULD HAVE COME DOWN THE CHIMNEY!

PRESENTS FORM 3

GRANDPA

WANTED

FOR CHRISTMAS

REWARD
1000 LAUGHS

The battle between The Jocks and The Geordies started 'way back in 1975 and even Christmas doesn't stop them fighting — the only gifts they give are a snowball on the head or a good duffing-up!

HA·HA·HAPPY NEW YEAR!

THE LAUGHTER BARRIERS CERTAINLY CAME DOWN FOR THIS END-OF-THE-YEAR KORKY PAGE, WHEN HE MADE SURE NO ONE TOOK 'OFFENCE'!

Even animals can have fun celebrating the coming of a new year — you're sure to be bamboozled at what the residents of Bamboo Town get up to in this page from the Dandy of the early '40s.

THE BASH STREET KIDS

DING!   DONG!   DING!   DONG!

IN BASH STREET STEEPLE ON DEC. 30th.—

OK, BOYS. THAT'S ENOUGH BELL-RINGING PRACTICE. YOU CAN GO HOME NOW. BUT REMEMBER —

BELL MUSIC PULL! TUG! PULL!

DEAR, OH, DEAR! THEY WON'T BE ABLE TO RING THE BELLS FOR THE NEW YEAR CELEBRATIONS NOW!

HEH! HEH! THAT'LL TEACH 'EM A LESSON!

I SURRENDER!

AT BASH STREET SCHOOL—
YOUR ROUGH CLASS BASHED MY BELL-RINGERS, SO THEY'LL HAVE TO RING THE STEEPLE BELLS NOW!

CLANG!

SO—

LATER— YOU BONE-BRAINED BEETLES! I DIDN'T MEAN YOU TO RING DOOR-BELLS — HOI! COME BACK HERE!

HE MUST HAVE MEANT SOME OTHER KIND OF BELLS, KIDS!

Class IIB

TEN MINUTES LATER—

STOP THAT NOISE!

ARE THESE THE SORT OF BELLS YOU MEANT, TEACHER?

BLOB STREET SCHOOL BELL

CLANG!   DONG!   DONG! DONG!   TING!   TRING!   TING!

FIRE BRIGADE

BATHING BELLE

TYPE WRITER

CLANK! CLANK!   TING! TING!

THE COMBINED WEIGHTS OF PLUG AND FATTY ARE TOO MUCH FOR POOR OL' "BIG BONG"!

BIG BONG

BO1-01- OI-OING!

GOOD GRIEF! THE CLAPPER OF THE BELL'S SHATTERED ON SMIFFY'S NUT!

CADOING!

YOU GOON! YOU'VE RUINED EVERYTHING! WE CAN'T RING IN THE NEW YEAR WITHOUT "BIG BONG," UNLESS — COME WITH ME, SMIFFY, M'BOY!

OOOYAH!

MIDNIGHT NEW YEAR'S

BIG BONG!
DING! DONG! DING! DONG!

HOW DID TEACHER MANAGE TO THE BELL IN TIME

GRANDPA

This large inflatable figure of Santa Claus was on show in Germany a few years ago . . . hey, what's that at the side of the picture . . .?